The INCREDIBLE
JOURNEY through the
HUMAN BODY

Nicholas Harris

D1421312

BigFish

www.bigfishonline.co.uk

• CONTENTS •

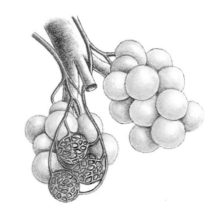

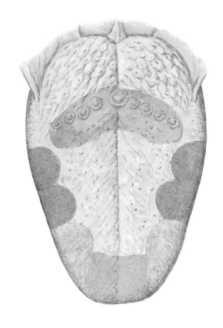

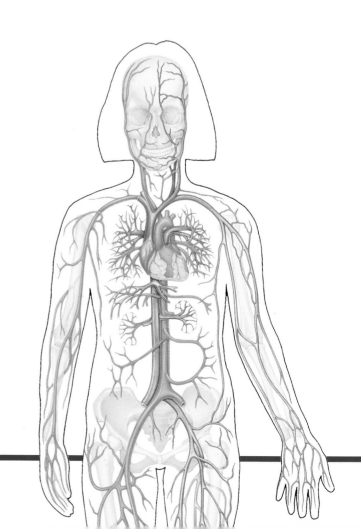

INTRODUCTION

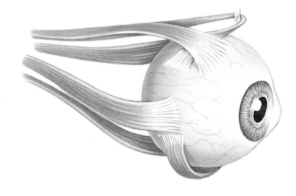

THE HUMAN BODY is, like all living things, an amazing natural creation. Given food and water, oxygen and warmth, it can grow from a baby to an adult, walk, talk, feel, think, and produce more of its own kind. All this is achieved by a collection of flesh, bone, blood and organs—about two-thirds of which is made up of just water. The parts of the body are, however, perfectly designed to act together in an incredibly complex way, making you the clever and agile human being you are!

You may go through your whole life without ever having seen what your own insides—an essential part of *you*—look like. Nowadays, using modern machines, doctors can view your internal organs without having to perform a surgical operation. And some foresee the invention of microscopic machines in the future that will be able to travel around the insides of the blood vessels, checking for any disorders. But nothing could compare with the exciting prospect of being able to go and see for yourself—the imaginary journey that we make in the following pages.

This journey takes us through some fantastic "landscapes". Explore, for example, the cavernous, slimy-walled, churning stomach, the winding tunnel of the intestines with walls made of millions of tiny "fingers", or the tangle of billions of tiny threads inside the brain. And come prepared for a long trip. The blood vessels stretch for 96,000 kilometres, or more than twice the distance round the Earth!

THE HUMAN BODY

ON OUR JOURNEY, we shall see what the body's organs, its working parts, look like from the inside. Different groups of organs work together in systems to keep the body going. For example, the blood, the blood vessels (arteries and veins) and the heart together form the circulatory system, which carries nutrients and oxygen to all parts of the body, and collects waste for removal. As well as the circulatory system, we shall be travelling through the digestive, respiratory (breathing), excretory (waste disposal) and nervous systems.

To make our journey, it will be necessary to shrink to a very small size. At its narrowest, the digestive system is only 2.5 centimetres wide. But we must be microscopically tiny to travel in the bloodstream, as the capillaries, the narrowest blood vessels, have a diameter of only one hundredth of a millimetre.

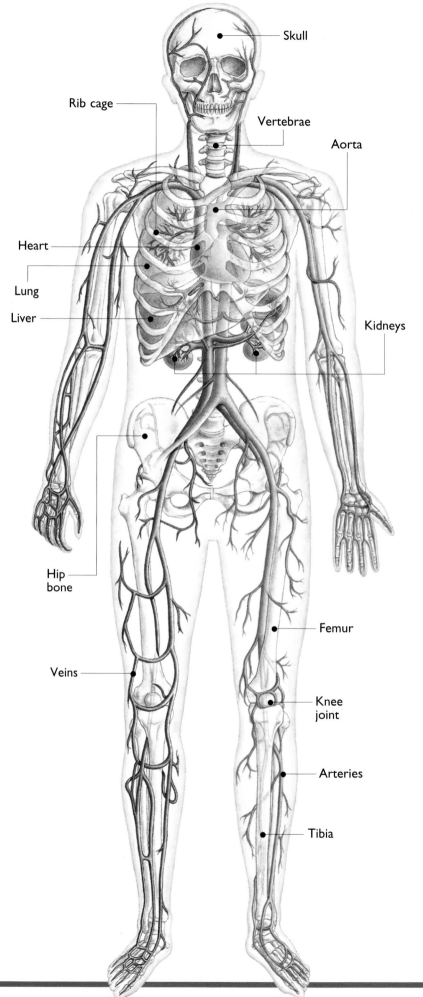

Skull
Rib cage
Vertebrae
Aorta
Heart
Lung
Liver
Kidneys
Hip bone
Femur
Veins
Knee joint
Arteries
Tibia

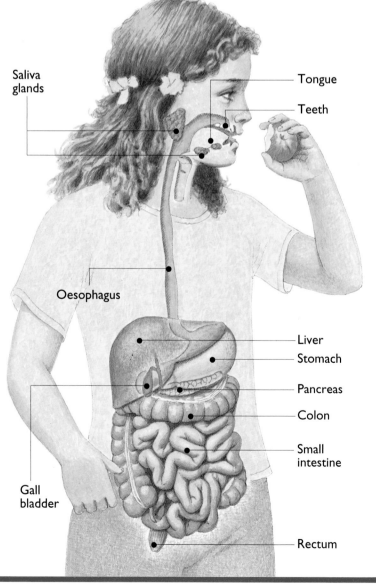

Saliva glands
Tongue
Teeth
Oesophagus
Liver
Stomach
Pancreas
Colon
Small intestine
Gall bladder
Rectum

Our journey begins at the mouth, the entrance to the digestive system. Here your food is mashed up by the teeth and moistened by saliva, before being pushed down the oesophagus. We follow the food along this stretchy tube, from where we emerge into the stomach. Here the food is churned up and mixed with digestive juices, then forced into the intestines. We pick our way through this long, tightly coiled tube, before passing into the bloodstream. We travel to the liver, where the nutrients from the food are extracted from the blood, then on to the heart, the circulatory system's pump. We accompany the blood cells to the lungs, where we pick up oxygen and unload carbon dioxide. Then the blood system takes us through the kidneys, which filter out waste substances. From there, we travel to the brain, the hub of the nervous system, finally riding the optic nerve to the eye, our journey's end.

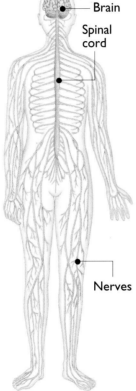

Brain
Spinal cord
Nerves

The body's nerves *(shown above, in yellow)* connect the organs and muscles with the brain, most of them via the spinal cord.

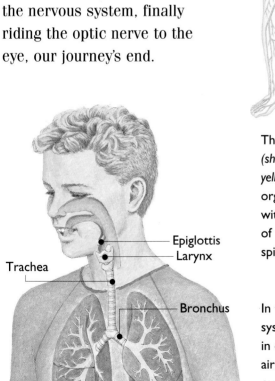

Epiglottis
Larynx
Trachea
Bronchus
Lungs

In the respiratory system, we breathe in oxygen from the air. Inside the lungs, oxygen is passed to the blood, while carbon dioxide, a waste gas, goes the opposite way.

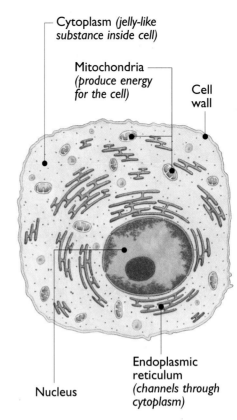

Cytoplasm *(jelly-like substance inside cell)*
Mitochondria *(produce energy for the cell)*
Cell wall
Endoplasmic reticulum *(channels through cytoplasm)*
Nucleus

Our bodies are made up of tiny "bricks", known as cells. There are more than 75 million million of them. Different kinds, for example, blood cells, nerve cells and liver cells, are all designed for different jobs, but all have a similar structure. At the centre is the nucleus, packed with chromosomes, tightly-wound strands of a substance called DNA. These contain the genes, a kind of instruction manual containing all the information necessary to create the body in a certain way.

The organs that make up the body's internal systems are protected by a strong framework of bone called the skeleton. The bones are connected to one another by joints which allow them to move. Every bone and joint has a different purpose. The skull and rib cage, for example, surround and protect the organs, while the 27 bones in the hand permit great dexterity.

Muscles *(shown right)* provide the power for movement. They are bands of tissue connected to the bones by tough cords called tendons. The brain gives the muscles a signal to contract (shorten), pulling a bone into position.

Wrapped around your organs, bones and muscles is the skin, the body's waterproof outer wrapping. The skin protects the body from harmful rays, helps control the body temperature and is extremely sensitive to touch and pain.

• MOUTH •

THE MOUTH is the gateway to our journey. It is the opening to the digestive tract, an 11-metre-long tube that runs all the way to the rectum, via the oesophagus, stomach and the tightly-coiled intestines. But only the indigestible parts of food we eat will travel the full length of the digestive tract. The digestible parts—the nutrients—will be absorbed into the bloodstream.

If you were a small piece of food, the mouth would look like a giant cavern. Rows of teeth, hard, bone-like structures embedded in the sockets of the jaws, rim the entrance. The teeth's job is to bite off chunks of food and grind them up into smaller pieces. Meanwhile, the lips press together to stop food falling out. Next the tongue, a strip of muscle attached to the lower jaw, moves the food around the

mouth and rolls it into balls ready for swallowing.

Saliva, a slippery liquid produced by glands under the tongue, in the neck and at the back of the throat, mixes with the chewed-up food to make it soft and mushy. You produce nearly two litres of saliva every day. It kills off some of the germs in the food, and it contains an enzyme (a substance that allows important chemical reactions to take place inside the body) that starts the process of digestion. Saliva also acts as a lubricant, helps you swallow, and allows you to taste. This is because the taste buds on the tongue *(see below)* respond only to liquids.

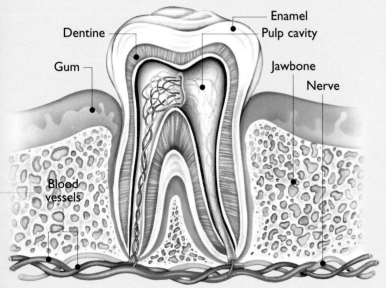

THE WISDOM TEETH DO NOT APPEAR UNTIL YOU ARE AN ADULT—WHEN YOU ARE SUPPOSED TO BE WISE • THE LIPS ACTUALLY EXTEND FROM THE LOWEST PART OF THE NOSE TO THE CHIN •

Enamel
Pulp cavity
Dentine
Gum
Jawbone
Nerve
Blood vessels

A tooth's roots are embedded deep into the jawbone. The tooth is made of dentine, a hard, bone-like material. The hollow interior, called the pulp cavity, contains minute blood vessels and nerves. Above the gum, the tooth is coated with enamel. This is the hardest substance in the body, but even this may be eaten away by acids made by bacteria from food left on or between the teeth. Different teeth have different jobs. The incisors slice up the food with their wide edges, while the canines tear it up. Molars and pre-molars crush and chew the food.

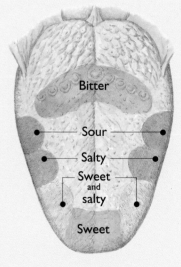

Bitter
Sour
Salty
Sweet and salty
Sweet

Thousands of tiny bumps on the tongue carry taste buds, which enable you to taste your food. Different parts of the tongue sense different flavours. Hundreds of different tastes are made up of combinations of four basic ones: bitter, sour, salty and sweet.

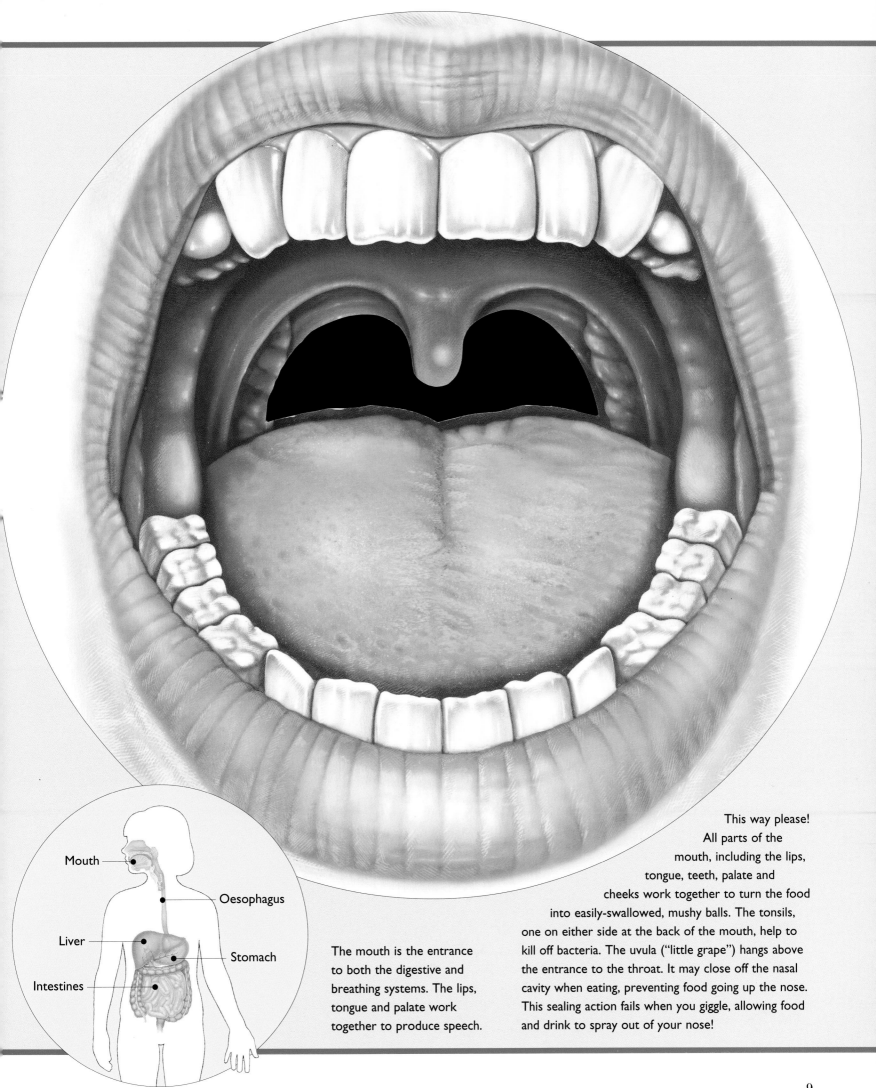

The mouth is the entrance to both the digestive and breathing systems. The lips, tongue and palate work together to produce speech.

This way please! All parts of the mouth, including the lips, tongue, teeth, palate and cheeks work together to turn the food into easily-swallowed, mushy balls. The tonsils, one on either side at the back of the mouth, help to kill off bacteria. The uvula ("little grape") hangs above the entrance to the throat. It may close off the nasal cavity when eating, preventing food going up the nose. This sealing action fails when you giggle, allowing food and drink to spray out of your nose!

Mouth

Oesophagus

Liver

Stomach

Intestines

WHEN THE FOOD has been sufficiently chewed, moistened and softened in the mouth, the tongue pushes the ball, or bolus, of food against the palate and into the throat. Your food now begins the next stage of its journey through the digestive system. It is squeezed down a stretchy tube about 25 centimetres long and two-and-a-half centimetres in diameter (the narrowest part of the digestive system) called the oesophagus.

The chewing and moistening process in the mouth has reduced the food to a mushy texture. The walls of the oesophagus are coated with mucus, a thick, slippery liquid that helps food slide down smoothly. The squeezing action of the muscle just behind the walls forces the food on its way. The journey from mouth to stomach takes about five seconds.

There is no need to think about swallowing. Your body does it for you in what is called a reflex action. Muscles go to work forcing the bolus down, while at the same time preventing it from going back into the mouth or even up your nose. A flap of tissue, called the epiglottis, folds over to close off the entrance to the trachea (windpipe). This makes sure that the food goes the right way—down the oesophagus to the stomach, not down the trachea. If the epiglottis does not close in time, violent coughing automatically ensures the food is forced out immediately.

LIQUID MAY TAKE ONLY 1-2 SECONDS TO PASS DOWN THE OESOPHAGUS (ABOUT 0.7 KM PER HOUR) • STOMACH ACIDS SOMETIMES FLOW BACK INTO THE OESOPHAGUS, CAUSING INDIGESTION

When swallowing *(below)*, the soft palate moves up to block off the nose. The epiglottis closes off the trachea.

Bolus
Soft palate
Throat
Oesophagus
Tongue
Epiglottis
Trachea

Soft palate
Bolus passes into oesophagus
Tongue
Epiglottis
Trachea

A bolus does not move down through the oesophagus of its own accord. It is pushed along by muscles. This is called peristalsis *(right)*. Muscles behind the bolus contract (pinch together) pushing it onwards (1) while the muscles ahead of it relax to allow it space (2). As the bolus moves forwards, these relaxed muscles then contract and the process is repeated (3). These muscular movements make it possible to swallow while upside down. Your brain controls peristalsis, although it is an automatic process.

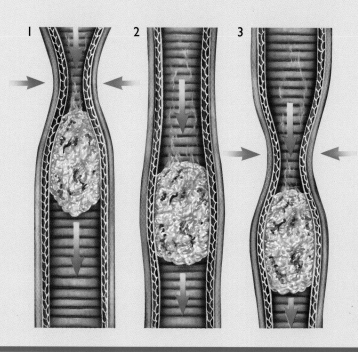

1   2   3

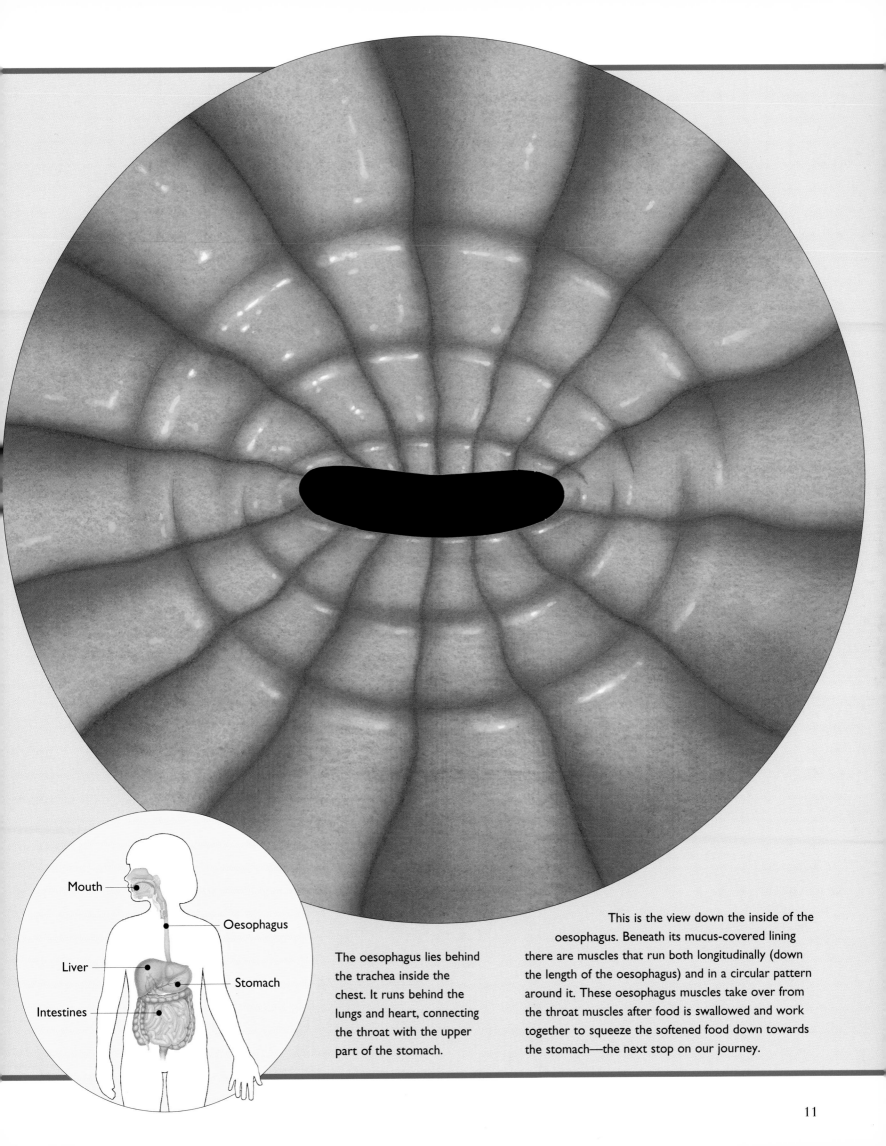

Mouth

Oesophagus

Liver

Stomach

Intestines

The oesophagus lies behind the trachea inside the chest. It runs behind the lungs and heart, connecting the throat with the upper part of the stomach.

This is the view down the inside of the oesophagus. Beneath its mucus-covered lining there are muscles that run both longitudinally (down the length of the oesophagus) and in a circular pattern around it. These oesophagus muscles take over from the throat muscles after food is swallowed and work together to squeeze the softened food down towards the stomach—the next stop on our journey.

IT TAKES only a few seconds to reach the stomach from the mouth—but we may be in here for two to three hours. The widest part of the digestive tract, the stomach is a J-shaped, muscle-walled bag that can contain about 1.5 litres of food and drink. The stretchy lining of the stomach allows it to grow bigger the more you eat—up to a limit!

We enter the stomach through a ring of muscle called a sphincter. This opens to let food in, then closes to stop stomach juices from going back up the oesophagus.

Stomach muscles squeeze and churn up the food that arrives in the stomach. At the same time the food is mixed with acid and enzymes, chemicals that help break down food into a digestible form. The result is a thick mush called chyme.

Sugary foods break down quickest, fatty foods slowest. Most of the bacteria that may be in the food are killed off by the acid in the stomach.

In fact, the acid and enzymes are so strong that the stomach needs to be prevented from digesting itself (the acid is powerful enough to dissolve the metal zinc). A thick layer of slime called mucus on the stomach wall does this job. Every minute, about half a million cells of the stomach lining die and must be replaced immediately.

The soft, gooey food mixture is now ready to pass along the digestive tract. Gradually, the chyme is squeezed through another sphincter at the lower end of the stomach and into the intestines.

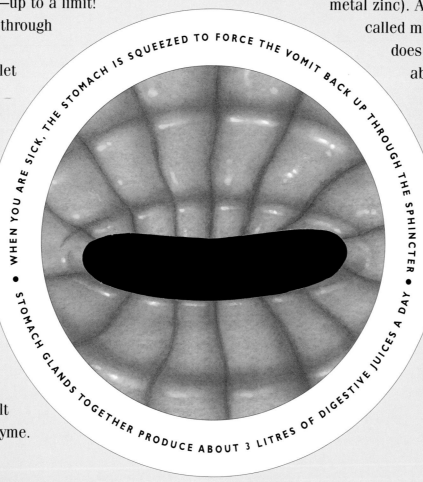

WHEN YOU ARE SICK, THE STOMACH IS SQUEEZED TO FORCE THE VOMIT BACK UP THROUGH THE SPHINCTER • STOMACH GLANDS TOGETHER PRODUCE ABOUT 3 LITRES OF DIGESTIVE JUICES A DAY •

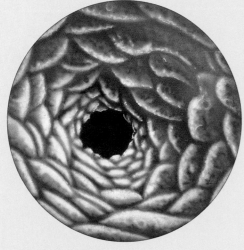

This is a greatly magnified view of part of the stomach wall. The deep hole is the opening to a tiny gland that produces acid and enzymes (digestive juices) which pour out over the food.

1

2

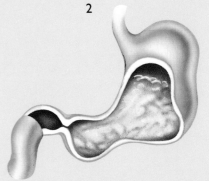

3

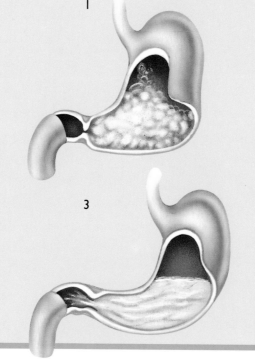

This sequence shows the workings of the stomach. When food arrives in the stomach from the oesophagus (1), it is broken down by chemicals and the churning action of the stomach (2). The food becomes a lumpy soup called chyme. This mixture is pushed out through the lower stomach (3).

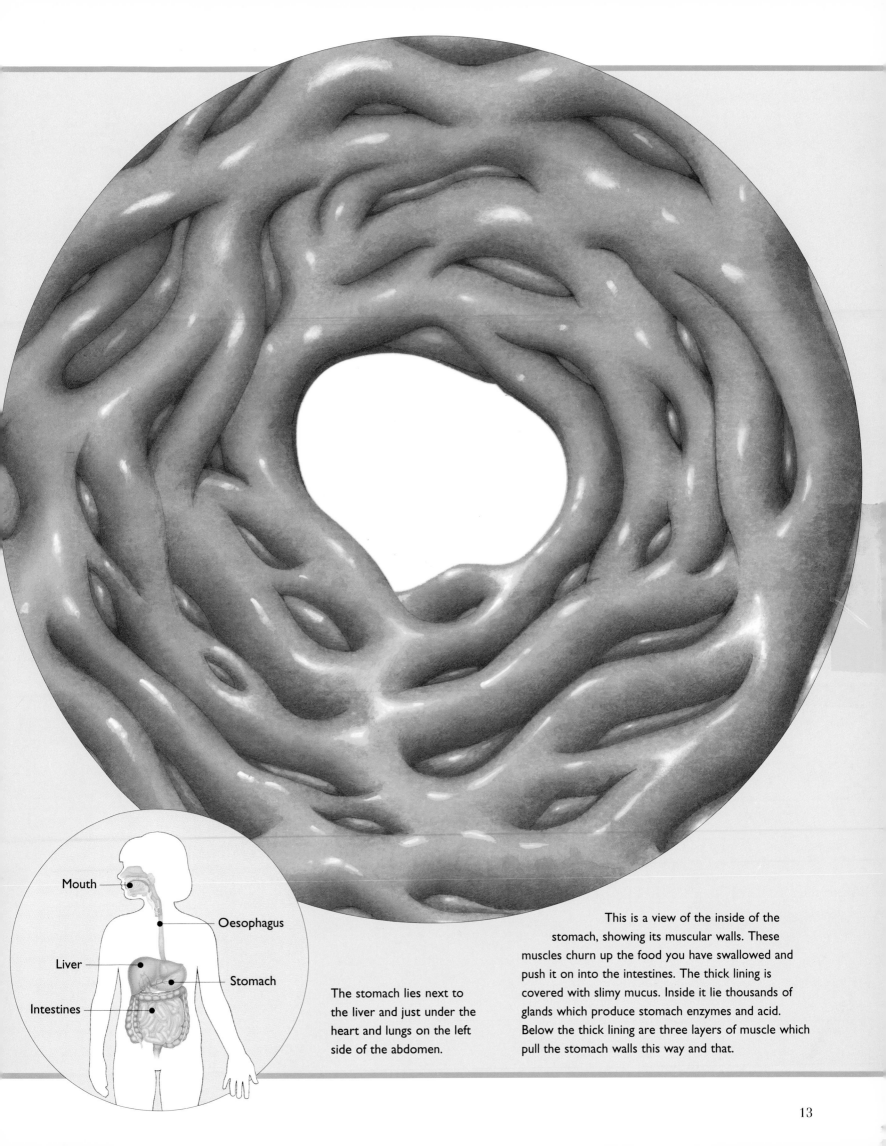

The stomach lies next to the liver and just under the heart and lungs on the left side of the abdomen.

This is a view of the inside of the stomach, showing its muscular walls. These muscles churn up the food you have swallowed and push it on into the intestines. The thick lining is covered with slimy mucus. Inside it lie thousands of glands which produce stomach enzymes and acid. Below the thick lining are three layers of muscle which pull the stomach walls this way and that.

Mouth

Oesophagus

Liver

Stomach

Intestines

WE ARE NOW inside the intestines, the place where all the useful substances, called nutrients, in your food are absorbed into the bloodstream. The small intestine is a tube, folded up many times over inside the abdomen—the place we often call our "tummy". The tube is only three-and-a-half centimetres wide but it is fully seven metres long, or about twice the length of a family car! The liquid slush that your food has become will creep along the small intestine over the course of four hours or so.

The walls of the small intestine are lined with millions of tiny "fingers", called villi, each one about half a millimetre long. They make the surface area of the walls much greater than if they were smooth. The surface area actually measures an amazing 350 square metres—about

the same as a basketball court. The villi are specially designed to absorb nutrients. Inside each villus there is a network of extremely fine tubes called blood capillaries. The walls between the capillaries and the small intestine are very thin. They allow the nutrients to pass easily from the intestines into the blood. Not all the food we eat gets into the bloodstream. Waste material the villi cannot absorb (mostly plant fibre and harmless bacteria) together with water travel on to the large intestine, or colon. Here, most of the water is absorbed back into the blood. The solid material that is left behind collects in the rectum. It is finally ejected from the body when we go to the lavatory.

• FOOD TAKES 18–24 HOURS TO TRAVEL FROM THE STOMACH ALONG THE INTESTINES TO THE RECTUM • THE APPENDIX, THE "TAIL END" OF THE LARGE INTESTINE HAS NO KNOWN USE

Our bodies need nutrients—fats, carbohydrates, proteins, vitamins and minerals—to keep healthy. All are absorbed in the intestines. Proteins, found in meat, fish, milk and green vegetables, help to build and repair body parts. Fats, from meat and dairy foods, and carbohydrates, found in bread, pasta and potatoes, provide energy. Vitamins and minerals are needed for good health. Iron, for example, found in meat and vegetables, is needed for the blood. Fibre, contained in fruit, vegetables and bread, helps the digestive system to work.

Fats

Iron (a mineral)

Fibre

Carbohydrates

Proteins

Vitamin A

This is a cross-section through a villus *(below)*, one of millions that line the walls of the small intestine. The surface of the villus is itself lined with thousands of microvilli, like the bristles on a brush.

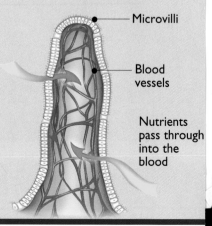

Microvilli

Blood vessels

Nutrients pass through into the blood

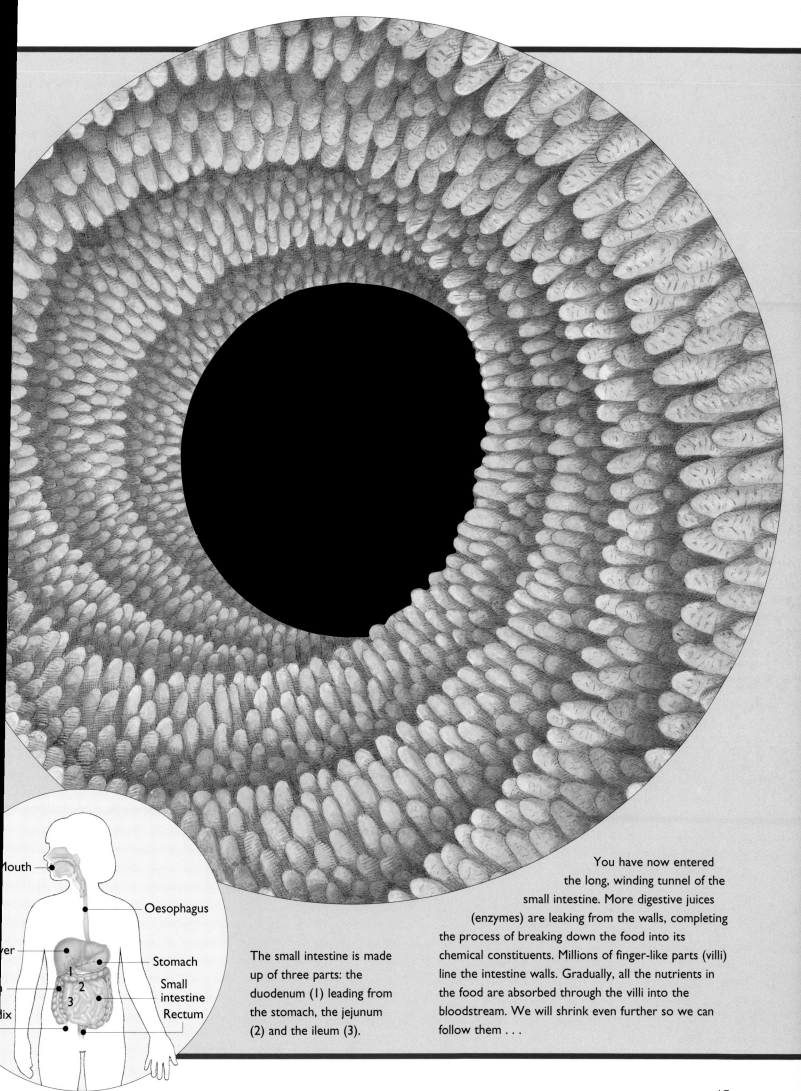

Mouth

Oesophagus

Stomach

Small intestine

Rectum

The small intestine is made up of three parts: the duodenum (1) leading from the stomach, the jejunum (2) and the ileum (3).

You have now entered the long, winding tunnel of the small intestine. More digestive juices (enzymes) are leaking from the walls, completing the process of breaking down the food into its chemical constituents. Millions of finger-like parts (villi) line the intestine walls. Gradually, all the nutrients in the food are absorbed through the villi into the bloodstream. We will shrink even further so we can follow them . . .

15

WE ARE NOW inside a blood capillary. The walls are extremely thin, enabling vital substances in the blood—including oxygen and nutrients—to seep through into the body's cells, while carbon dioxide and other waste can pass the other way.

The task of picking up oxygen from the lungs and carrying it to the body's cells is done by the red blood cells. They contain a substance called haemoglobin which combines very quickly with oxygen. White blood cells are designed to defend the body against infection by bacteria. This they do by engulfing them, or by making substances to destroy them or counter their effects. Also found in the blood are tiny particles called

platelets, which clot blood in wounds. The cells platelets are all carried in a yellowish, watery li called plasma. Nutrients and other substances n by the body's cells are dissolved in the plasma. Together with the red blood cells, the plasma pic waste carbon dioxide and returns it to the

All the blood vessels in the hu body are basically hollow tu Arteries, which carry blo with fresh oxygen and nutrients from the to the body's vari organs, have thi elastic walls because the b running throu them is pump under pressur Veins carry th blood, togethe with carbon dic and other waste from the organs b to the heart. Their are thinner because th is less pressure.

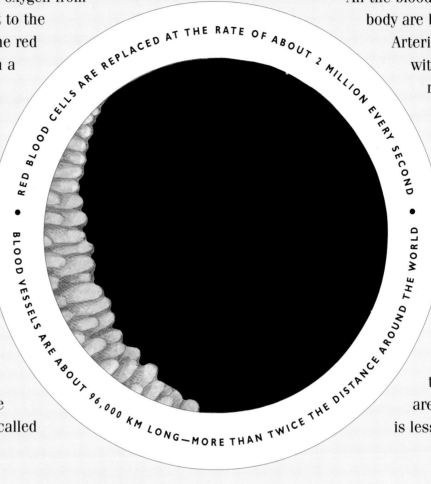

RED BLOOD CELLS ARE REPLACED AT THE RATE OF ABOUT 2 MILLION EVERY SECOND • BLOOD VESSELS ARE ABOUT 96,000 KM LONG—MORE THAN TWICE THE DISTANCE AROUND THE WORLD •

Both red and white blood cells and platelets are made in the marrow, a jelly-like substance found in the spongy insides of our bones *(left)*. In children, whose bones are growing quickly and contain a large amount of marrow, about 200 billion blood cells are produced every day. The new cells enter the bloodstream through the blood vessels that run through the bones. The cells have a life of about 120 days on average. The blood cells are finally carried to the spleen, liver or bone marrow where they are destroyed.

— Bone marrow

— Surface of bone

Artery

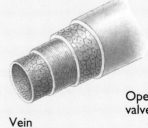

Vein

Both arteries and veins *(left)* several layers of muscle and elastic tissue. Arteries are th because they must withstand higher pressure. The larger v have valves inside them *(belo* that open and close rather li canal locks. The valves ensur the flow of blood is constant that it cannot leak back.

Open valve

Closed valve

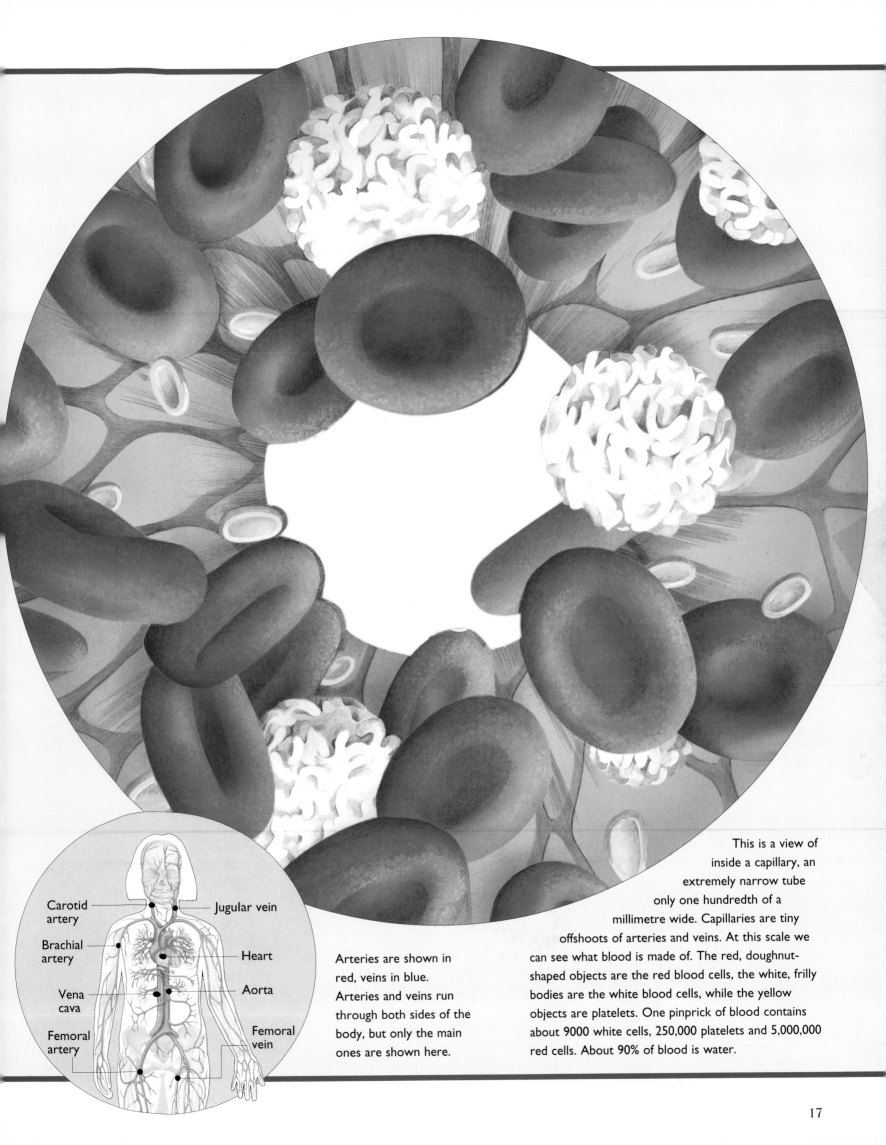

Carotid artery

Jugular vein

Brachial artery

Heart

Vena cava

Aorta

Femoral artery

Femoral vein

Arteries are shown in red, veins in blue. Arteries and veins run through both sides of the body, but only the main ones are shown here.

This is a view of inside a capillary, an extremely narrow tube only one hundredth of a millimetre wide. Capillaries are tiny offshoots of arteries and veins. At this scale we can see what blood is made of. The red, doughnut-shaped objects are the red blood cells, the white, frilly bodies are the white blood cells, while the yellow objects are platelets. One pinprick of blood contains about 9000 white cells, 250,000 platelets and 5,000,000 red cells. About 90% of blood is water.

• LIVER •

EVERY DROP OF BLOOD coming from the intestines must pass through the liver before it goes anywhere else. So the liver is the next stop on our journey. The largest organ in the human body after the skin, the liver has many tasks. Acting as a kind of food processor, it makes new chemicals from the nutrients it receives in the blood from the small intestine. It also acts as a waste disposal unit, removing substances the body does not need.

Nutrients are stored in the liver until they are required. If there is more glucose, for example, than the body needs, it will be changed into a substance called glycogen. As the body burns up energy, the liver changes glycogen back into energy-giving glucose and passes it on into the bloodstream.

Sometimes there are more amino acids, nutrients from foods rich in protein (meat, for example) than the body needs. The liver changes some of these into carbohydrates, to give energy, and the rest into a waste substance called urea, which goes to the kidneys *(see page 24)*, from where it leaves the body in urine.

The liver also collects up old, worn-out red blood cells and cleans out poisons, drugs, alcohol and other impurities from the bloodstream. Some of the chemical waste is turned into bile, which is stored in the gall bladder. This empties out back in the small intestine where it helps the digestive process by mixing with fats, enabling them to be taken into the bloodstream through the intestine walls.

• AT ANY ONE TIME, ABOUT A QUARTER OF YOUR BLOOD IS INSIDE YOUR LIVER BEING CLEANSED AND RE-STOCKED WITH GLUCOSE • THE LIVER COULD STILL FUNCTION EVEN IF 90% OF IT WERE REMOVED •

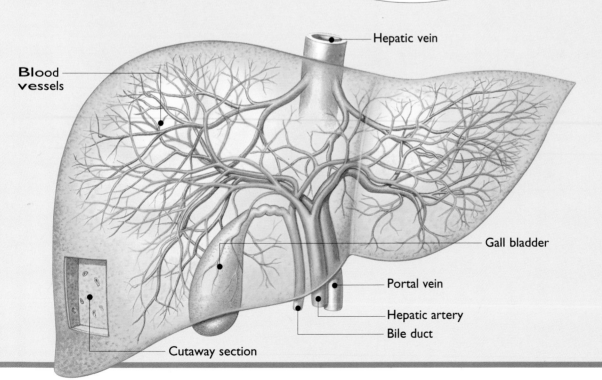

Blood vessels

Hepatic vein

Gall bladder

Portal vein

Hepatic artery

Bile duct

Cutaway section

How does the liver perform all its tasks? Blood from the intestines containing nutrients enters the liver through the portal vein. The blood is channelled into millions of branches which reach out into all parts of the liver. The organ is, itself, made up of millions of tiny, six-sided lobules containing the cells where all the processing and waste-disposal work is done. Blood passes through the lobules, and, once it is "treated", collects into a system of branches that take it to the hepatic vein, and from there on to the heart.

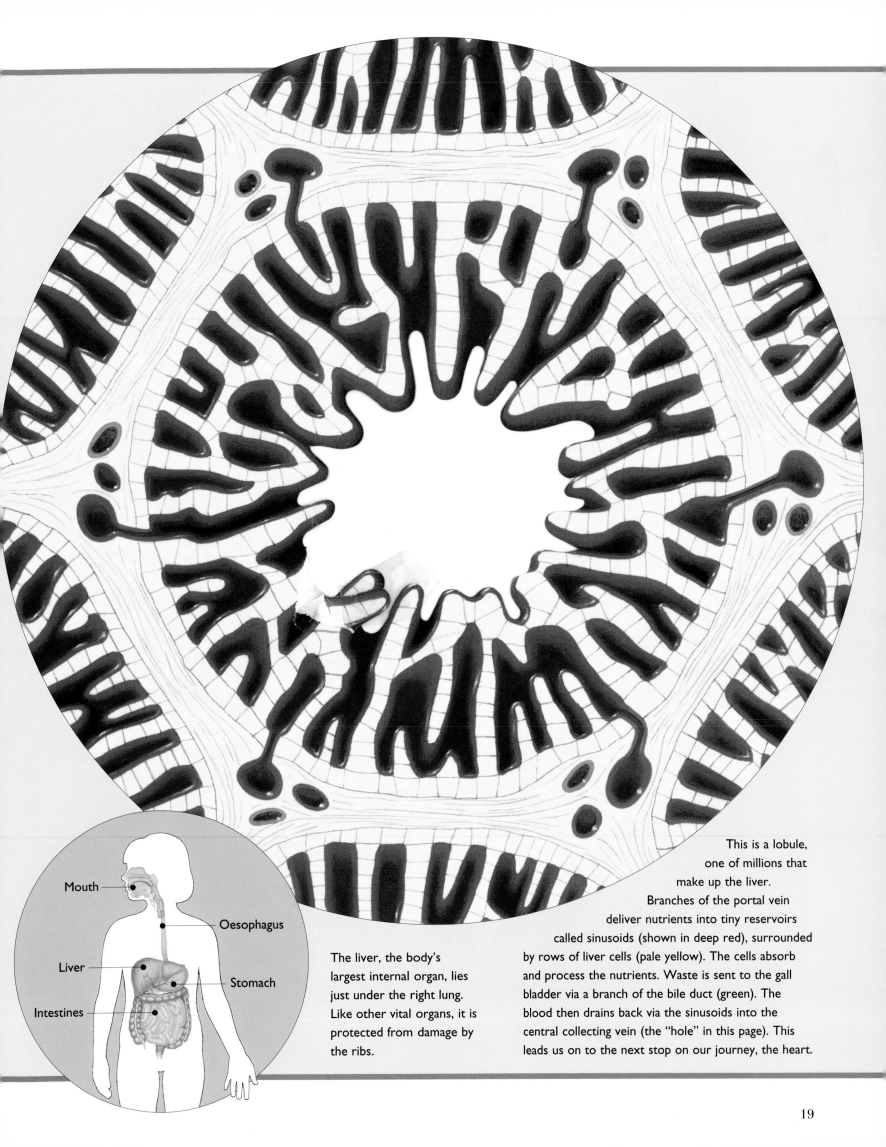

Mouth

Oesophagus

Liver

Stomach

Intestines

The liver, the body's largest internal organ, lies just under the right lung. Like other vital organs, it is protected from damage by the ribs.

This is a lobule, one of millions that make up the liver. Branches of the portal vein deliver nutrients into tiny reservoirs called sinusoids (shown in deep red), surrounded by rows of liver cells (pale yellow). The cells absorb and process the nutrients. Waste is sent to the gall bladder via a branch of the bile duct (green). The blood then drains back via the sinusoids into the central collecting vein (the "hole" in this page). This leads us on to the next stop on our journey, the heart.

THE HEPATIC VEIN carries us, together with its cargo of newly processed blood, into a larger vein called the vena cava, and from there to the heart. This fist-sized organ is made entirely of muscle and is incredibly powerful. Its job is to pump the blood around the body. It beats more than two billion times during the average life span and pumps about 340 litres of blood every hour—enough to fill a car's petrol tank every seven minutes.

Veins carry blood not only from the liver, but from all the body's muscles and tissues. There is very little oxygen left in this blood, so it must return to the lungs *(see page 22)* to pick up fresh oxygen. At the same time, blood that has already been to the lungs arrives in other veins, called the pulmonary veins. The heart muscles suck in the blood from both sources. Then, when it is full of blood, the heart squeezes inwards, pushing the oxygen-rich blood into the aorta and the oxygen-poor blood into the pulmonary arteries. The oxygen-rich blood travels along the aorta to arteries branching off to all parts of the body, while the oxygen-poor blood goes on to the lungs (the next stage of our journey).

The strong muscles of the heart pump the blood along at high pressure. This ensures that the flow of blood is sufficiently powerful to travel—against gravity—up to the brain *(see page 26).*

THE HEART OF A BLUE WHALE WEIGHS ABOUT THE SAME AS A SMALL CAR • THE HEART MAY BEAT MORE THAN 200 TIMES A MINUTE AFTER STRENUOUS EXERCISE

Aorta

Vena cava

Pulmonary artery

Left atrium

Pulmonary veins

Right atrium

Valve

Chordae tendinae

Left ventricle

Right ventricle

➡ Movement of oxygen-rich blood

➡ Movement of oxygen-poor blood

There are four chambers in the heart (left and right atria, left and right ventricles). Flaps, called valves, close to prevent blood flowing back once it has entered each chamber (the thumps of the valves closing is the heartbeat you can hear). The diagrams *(right)* show how the heart works. Blood arrives in the heart through the pulmonary veins from the lungs *(shown in red)*—the only veins in the body that carry oxygen-rich blood—and through the vena cava from the rest of the body *(shown in blue)*. By squeezing inwards, the heart pushes the blood out.

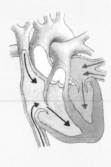

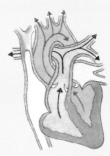

We are now inside one of the heart's chambers. This is a view looking down at the interior of a ventricle, one of the lower chambers and the hardest-working part of the heart. The cream-coloured surface is a valve, shown here held open by chords, known as the chordae tendinae (commonly known as heartstrings), which are themselves anchored to the base of the ventricle. Once a quantity of blood has passed through to the ventricle, the valve snaps shut behind it.

The heart lies at the centre of the blood transport system, for which it acts as a pump. All the blood vessels connect up to it.

A JOURNEY through the blood system must always lead us, via the heart—the body's central pumping station—to the lungs. The lungs are where blood, exhausted of oxygen that has been used to fuel the body's cells, takes on fresh supplies of oxygen. The cells use oxygen to burn up sugars and provide energy. This process produces a waste gas, carbon dioxide, so this must be off-loaded from the blood in the lungs at the same time.

The pulmonary artery takes us from the heart into the lungs: two large, spongy organs, made up almost entirely of a latticework of tubes. The artery immediately subdivides into millions of tiny branches called capillaries. Also leading into each lung is a tube called a bronchus. This is connected to the trachea (windpipe),

through whic[...] and nose. Th[...] millions of ti[...] of these ends[...] alveoli—each[...] capillar[...]

THERE ARE MORE THAN 300 MILLION ALVEOLI OR "AIR[...] • AT REST, YOU BREATHE IN ABOUT HALF A LITRE OF A[...]

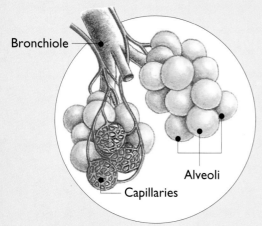

Bronchiole

Alveoli

Capillaries

Clustered like a bunch of grapes, the alveoli provide a huge surface area, allowing the exchange of oxygen and carbon dioxide to take place quickly and efficiently.

Inside the trachea is the voice box, or larynx. Two straps, the vocal cords, lie across it. They vibrate when air is breathed out, producing sounds that the mouth can form into words.

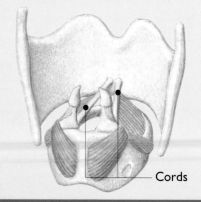

Cords

Heart

Veins

Arteries

The heart lies at the centre of the blood transport system, for which it acts as a pump. All the blood vessels connect up to it.

We are now inside one of the heart's chambers. This is a view looking down at the interior of a ventricle, one of the lower chambers and the hardest-working part of the heart. The cream-coloured surface is a valve, shown here held open by chords, known as the chordae tendinae (commonly known as heartstrings), which are themselves anchored to the base of the ventricle. Once a quantity of blood has passed through to the ventricle, the valve snaps shut behind it.

• LUNGS •

A JOURNEY through the blood system must always lead us, via the heart—the body's central pumping station—to the lungs. The lungs are where blood, exhausted of oxygen that has been used to fuel the body's cells, takes on fresh supplies of oxygen. The cells use oxygen to burn up sugars and provide energy. This process produces a waste gas, carbon dioxide, so this must be off-loaded from the blood in the lungs at the same time.

The pulmonary artery takes us from the heart into the lungs: two large, spongy organs, made up almost entirely of a latticework of tubes. The artery immediately subdivides into millions of tiny branches called capillaries. Also leading into each lung is a tube called a bronchus. This is connected to the trachea (windpipe), through which air passes in and out via the mouth and nose. The bronchus is also subdivided into millions of tiny airways called bronchioles. Every one of these ends in a tiny cluster of air chambers called alveoli—each surrounded by a dense network of blood capillaries. The alveoli are the places where oxygen that we have breathed in, and which has travelled along the trachea, bronchus and bronchioles, seeps into the bloodstream. At the same time, carbon dioxide (and water vapour) in the blood escapes through the very thin walls of the alveoli into the bronchioles. When we breathe out, it travels in the opposite direction, exiting the body via the mouth and nose.

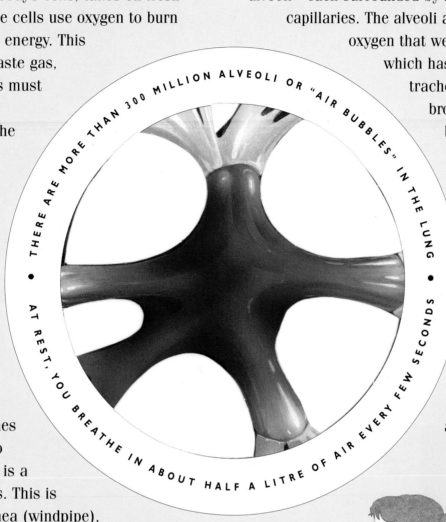

THERE ARE MORE THAN 300 MILLION ALVEOLI OR "AIR BUBBLES" IN THE LUNG • AT REST, YOU BREATHE IN ABOUT HALF A LITRE OF AIR EVERY FEW SECONDS

Bronchiole
Alveoli
Capillaries

Clustered like a bunch of grapes, the alveoli provide a huge surface area, allowing the exchange of oxygen and carbon dioxide to take place quickly and efficiently.

Inside the trachea is the voice box, or larynx. Two straps, the vocal cords, lie across it. They vibrate when air is breathed out, producing sounds that the mouth can form into words.

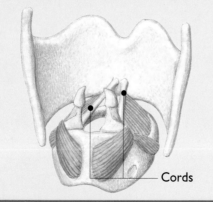

Cords

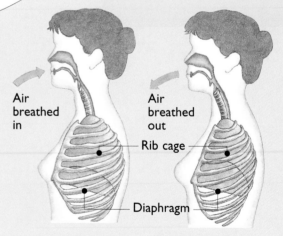

Air breathed in
Air breathed out
Rib cage
Diaphragm

To breathe in, the lung cavity is made bigger by being pulled down by the diaphragm (a sheet of muscle that lies underneath the lungs) and out by the rib muscles. Air is sucked in to fill the larger space. To breathe out, the muscles are relaxed, returning the lungs to their former size. This pushes the air out.

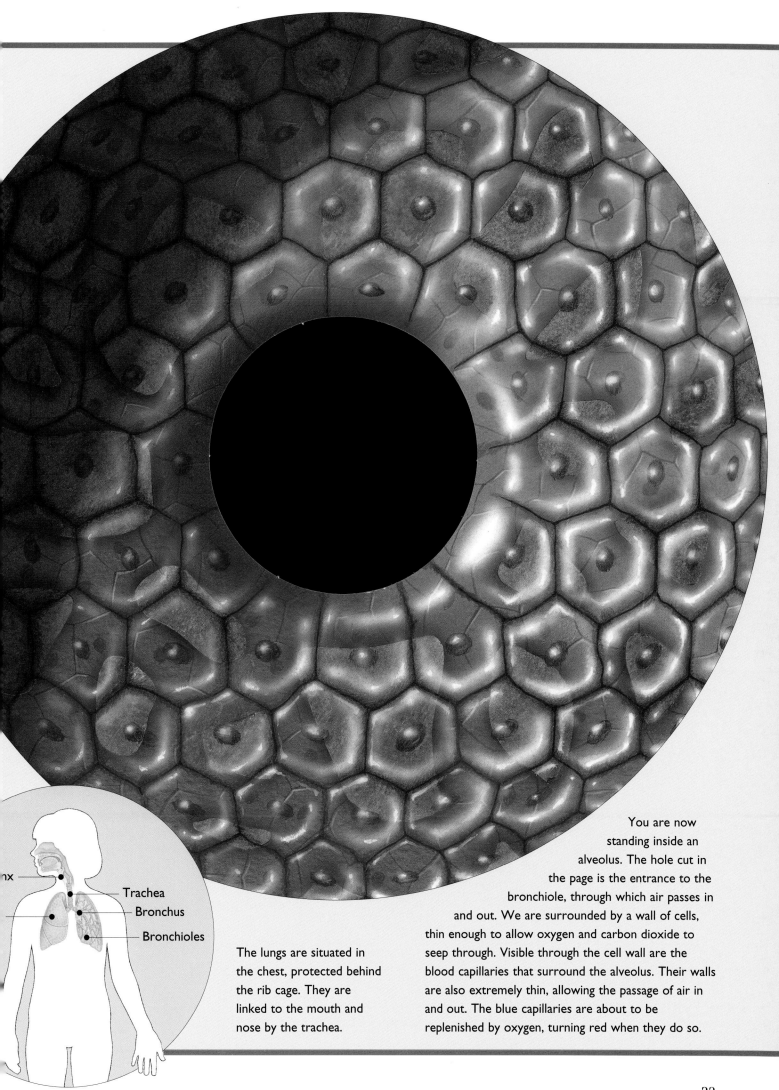

nx

Trachea

Bronchus

Bronchioles

The lungs are situated in the chest, protected behind the rib cage. They are linked to the mouth and nose by the trachea.

You are now standing inside an alveolus. The hole cut in the page is the entrance to the bronchiole, through which air passes in and out. We are surrounded by a wall of cells, thin enough to allow oxygen and carbon dioxide to seep through. Visible through the cell wall are the blood capillaries that surround the alveolus. Their walls are also extremely thin, allowing the passage of air in and out. The blue capillaries are about to be replenished by oxygen, turning red when they do so.

• KIDNEYS •

AN ARTERY from the heart takes us straight to one of two kidneys that you have in your body. Each kidney is about 11 centimetres long and shaped like a large bean. The kidneys act as the blood's washing machine: they take out all the substances in the blood that are not needed (including all the waste produced by the liver such as urea), allowing only useful substances to remain. They also control the levels of water and salts in the blood. The kidneys have an enormous work capacity, so that they can filter about one quarter of your entire bloodstream in about one minute.

Blood arrives at the kidneys from the heart via the renal artery under high pressure. The renal artery subdivides into smaller arteries, which pass into a dense mass of filter units called nephrons. Each kidney consists of more than a million nephrons. They e act as a sieve, allowing only water and waste dissolved in it to pass through, while holding bac proteins and blood cells that the body needs to k The dissolved waste, known as urine, trickl into the ureter, a tube that leads bladder.

Instead of trickling ou the body all the time, collects in the blad kind of storage ta As the bladder f (it can take up about 600 millilitres at maximum), th muscular wal expand until t brain tells the that the urine be released.

Meanwhile, the b cleansed of its was the kidneys, leaves by renal vein to continue it journey round the body.

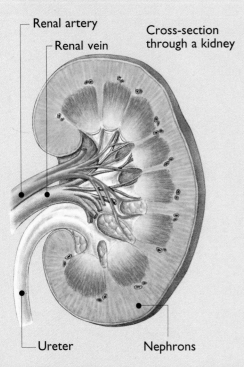

IF ALL THE KIDNEY'S TUBULES WERE LAID END TO END, THEY WOULD STRETCH FOR MORE THAN 60 METRES • ABOUT 165 LITRES OF FLUID FROM THE BLOOD PASSES THOUGH THE KIDNEYS IN ONE DAY •

Renal artery

Renal vein

Cross-section through a kidney

Ureter

Nephrons

Blood from the renal artery passes into a network of branches or capillaries, each of which passes through a nephron. There are two parts to every nephron: the glomerolus, a knot of tiny blood capillaries, and the tubule, where water and essential nutrients are re-absorbed into the blood. Water and waste pass from the blood in the glomerolus. Then, on its passage through the tubule, some of the water and any useful substances dissolved in it, pass back into the capillaries. Excess water, plus waste, continues on to the collecting tubule.

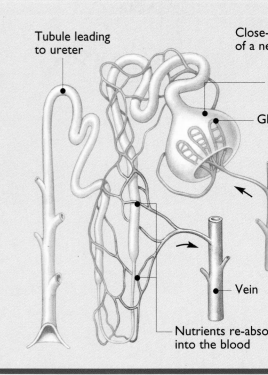

Tubule leading to ureter

Close-of a ne

Gl

Vein

Nutrients re-abso into the blood

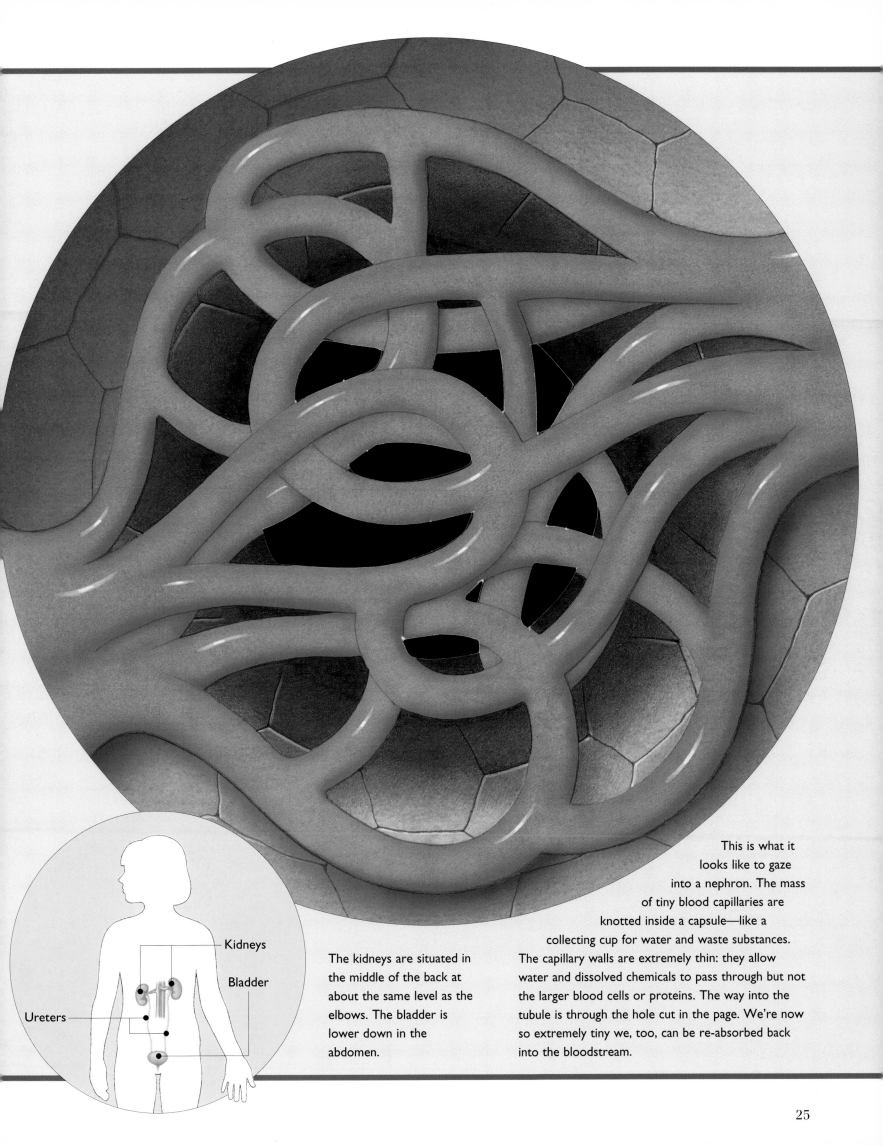

The kidneys are situated in the middle of the back at about the same level as the elbows. The bladder is lower down in the abdomen.

This is what it looks like to gaze into a nephron. The mass of tiny blood capillaries are knotted inside a capsule—like a collecting cup for water and waste substances. The capillary walls are extremely thin: they allow water and dissolved chemicals to pass through but not the larger blood cells or proteins. The way into the tubule is through the hole cut in the page. We're now so extremely tiny we, too, can be re-absorbed back into the bloodstream.

Kidneys

Bladder

Ureters

• BRAIN •

SOME of the largest blood vessels take us from the heart up through the neck and into the head where we reach the brain. Although the brain makes up just two per cent of the body's mass, it needs about a quarter of all the oxygen you breathe in. This is simply because it uses up so much more energy than other body cells.

The brain does, after all, have a very important job to perform. It acts as the control centre of the body. It sends out instructions for the way you move, decides the rate at which you breathe, how quickly the heart must beat and many other vital tasks. It also gives you your personality, decides how you think and stores information for recall later. To do this, the brain constantly takes in a vast amount of information, which it analyses, then acts upon.

The information the brain needs travels to it along an incredibly dense network of nerves. Nerves, bundles of thin, fibrous nerve cells, are like telephone wires, linking the brain to all parts of the body. There are billions of them, and most are linked to the spinal cord, a bundle as thick as your finger that runs along your backbone to the brain. Instructions from the brain travel in the opposite direction. Nerve signals from the eyes, ears and your other senses, such as taste, touch and smell, travel along nerves to the brain. There are also other sensors in the body that provide the brain with information about temperature, fluid levels, amounts of nutrients, and so on. The brain controls breathing, digestion, muscle co-ordination and all the other internal systems that keep you going automatically.

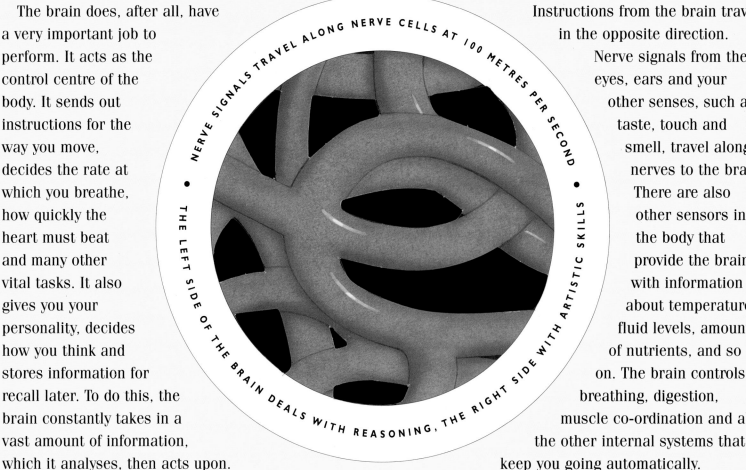

NERVE SIGNALS TRAVEL ALONG NERVE CELLS AT 100 METRES PER SECOND • THE LEFT SIDE OF THE BRAIN DEALS WITH REASONING, THE RIGHT SIDE WITH ARTISTIC SKILLS

The brain is divided into three main regions: the forebrain, the cerebellum and the brain stem. The chief part of the forebrain is the cerebrum, which makes up about 85% of the brain's mass. It is responsible for conscious thoughts and actions. Also part of the forebrain is the hypothalamus, which controls many of the body's automatic processes such as sleeping and eating. The cerebellum ensures that body movements are co-ordinated, while the brain stem monitors the heartbeat, breathing, blood pressure and other vital functions.

Hypothalamus

Cerebrum

Brain stem

Cerebellum

Cross-section through the brain

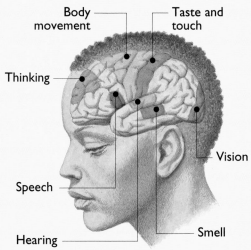

Body movement

Taste and touch

Thinking

Speech

Vision

Hearing

Smell

Certain areas of the cerebral cortex, the outer layer of the cerebrum, deal with particular functions.

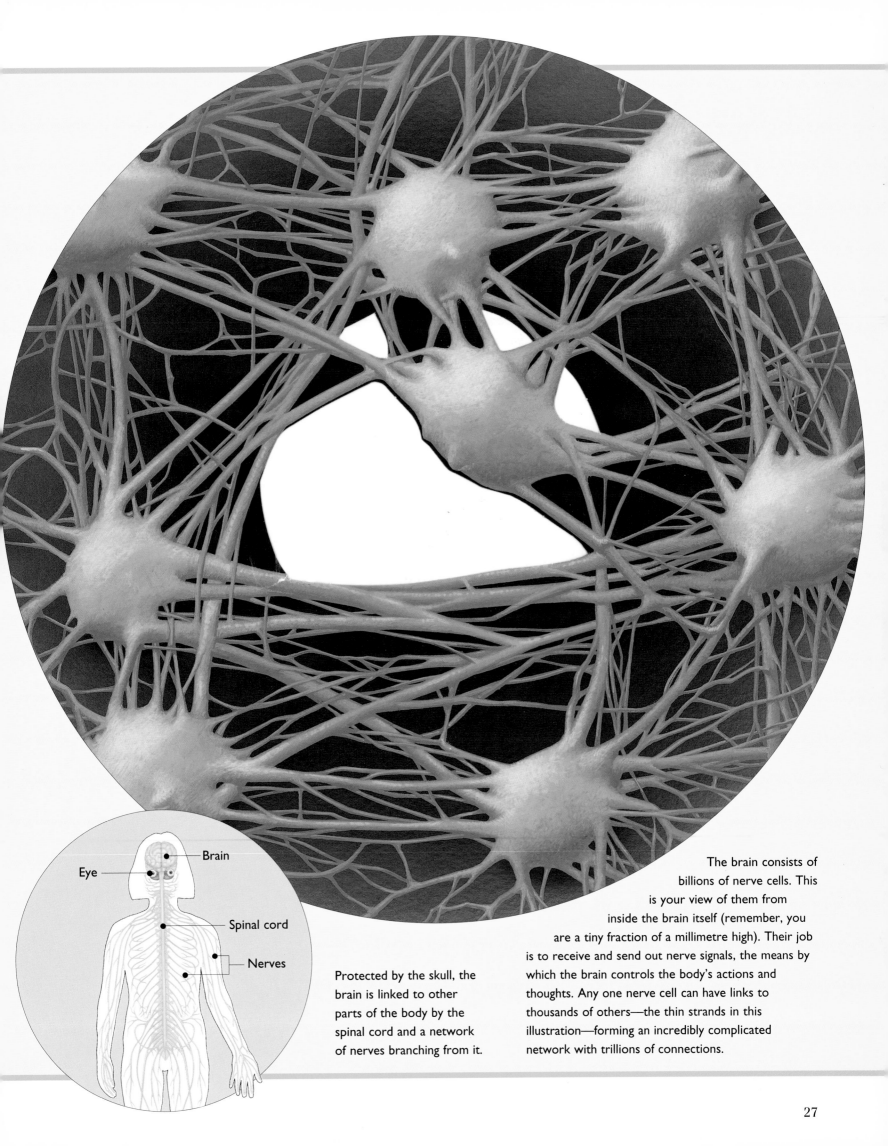

Brain

Eye

Spinal cord

Nerves

Protected by the skull, the brain is linked to other parts of the body by the spinal cord and a network of nerves branching from it.

The brain consists of billions of nerve cells. This is your view of them from inside the brain itself (remember, you are a tiny fraction of a millimetre high). Their job is to receive and send out nerve signals, the means by which the brain controls the body's actions and thoughts. Any one nerve cell can have links to thousands of others—the thin strands in this illustration—forming an incredibly complicated network with trillions of connections.

• EYE •

WE HAVE TRAVELLED along a nerve (the optic nerve) from the brain to reach the eye. We arrive at the back of the retina, the curved inside wall of the eyeball. The fovea, a region on the retina at the back of the eye, is the place where the eye best focuses images from the outside world. There, light-sensitive cells send signals back along the optic nerve (actually a bundle of about a million nerve cells) to the brain. Sight is the most important of our senses: around three-quarters of all information processed in the brain comes in through the eyes alone.

Light enters the eye through a transparent, domed window called the cornea at the front of the eye. This does most of the work of focusing images on to the retina. Only half a millimetre thick at the centre, its outer suface is the epithelium, a transparent continuation of the skin. Light passes through an opening, called the pupil, in the iris, the eye's coloured part. This is a ring of muscle that controls the size of the pupil. The iris works like the aperture on a camera: if too much light falls on the pupil, the pupil is reduced in size. If too little light enters, it grows larger. The pupil can vary in size from one to eight millimetres. The adjustment is automatic—it works without any conscious effort. Behind the iris there is a soft, elastic lens, which finely adjusts the sharpness of the image. The main body of the eye is filled with a clear, jelly-like substance called the vitreous humour. This gives the eye its shape and firmness.

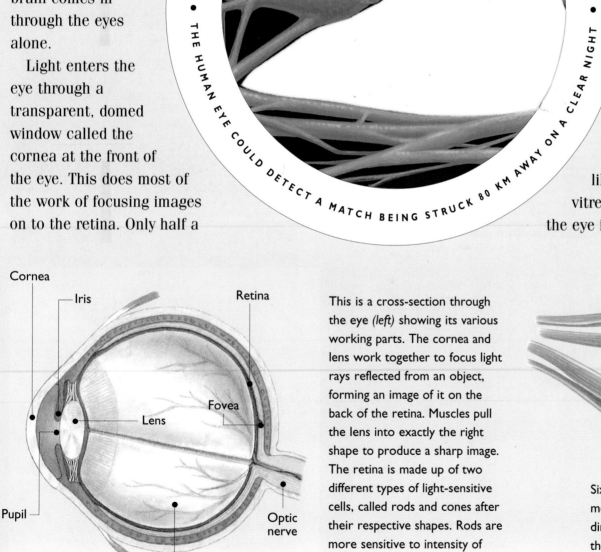

THE MUSCLES MOVE THE EYE ABOUT 100,000 TIMES A DAY, MOSTLY WHILE YOU ARE ASLEEP • THE HUMAN EYE COULD DETECT A MATCH BEING STRUCK 80 KM AWAY ON A CLEAR NIGHT •

This is a cross-section through the eye *(left)* showing its various working parts. The cornea and lens work together to focus light rays reflected from an object, forming an image of it on the back of the retina. Muscles pull the lens into exactly the right shape to produce a sharp image. The retina is made up of two different types of light-sensitive cells, called rods and cones after their respective shapes. Rods are more sensitive to intensity of light than to colour, which is the job of the cones.

Cornea
Iris
Retina
Fovea
Lens
Pupil
Optic nerve
Vitreous humour

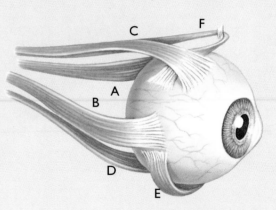

Six muscles work together to move the eyeball in different directions. Muscle A swivels it to the left, B to the right, C upwards and D downwards. Muscles E and F rotate the eyeball diagonally.

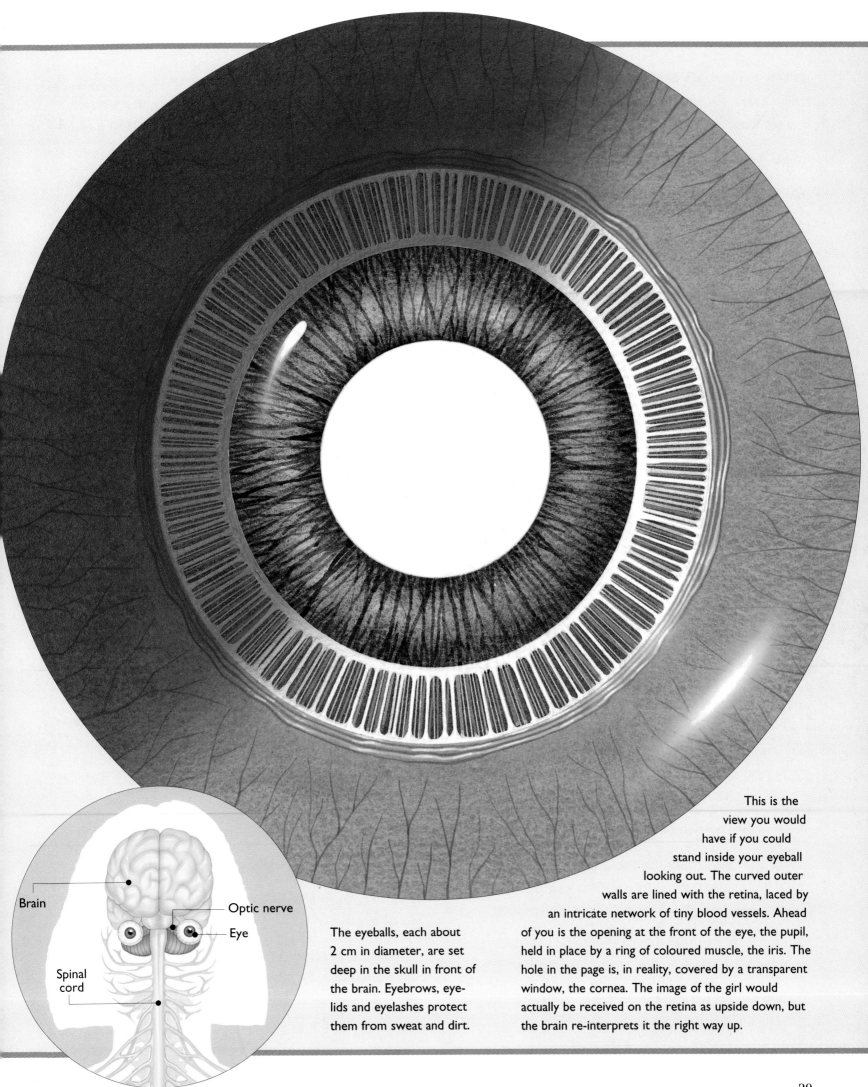

Brain

Optic nerve

Eye

Spinal cord

The eyeballs, each about 2 cm in diameter, are set deep in the skull in front of the brain. Eyebrows, eyelids and eyelashes protect them from sweat and dirt.

This is the view you would have if you could stand inside your eyeball looking out. The curved outer walls are lined with the retina, laced by an intricate network of tiny blood vessels. Ahead of you is the opening at the front of the eye, the pupil, held in place by a ring of coloured muscle, the iris. The hole in the page is, in reality, covered by a transparent window, the cornea. The image of the girl would actually be received on the retina as upside down, but the brain re-interprets it the right way up.

· GLOSSARY ·

Alveoli Tiny air sacs in the lungs where oxygen is taken up by the blood and carbon dioxide is released into the lungs and breathed out.

Amino acid A chemical that makes up proteins.

Artery A tube that carries blood away from the heart.

Bronchus The tube through which air passes from the trachea to each lung. Inside the lung, the bronchus subdivides into smaller branches called bronchioles.

Capillaries The smallest type of blood vessels, whose walls are the thickness of only one cell.

Carbohydrates Foods like sugars and starches which provide energy for the body.

Cell A tiny "building block" which makes up all the tissues in the human body—and in all living things, including plants. The blood provides it with nutrients and oxygen and removes waste from it.

Enzyme A substance, usually a kind of protein, that speeds up chemical reactions. There are many kinds, each performing a number of important jobs, such as helping to digest food and obtain energy from it.

Epiglottis A flap at the upper entrance of the trachea. It prevents food from passing down into the lungs.

Genes The instructions contained in the nucleus of every cell. They control the way in which all your cells are built, and so determine all your looks and characteristics.

Gland A body part that produces a useful substance inside the body, for example, sweat, saliva and digestive juices.

Glycogen A form of glucose (the main source of energy for the body's cells) that is stored in the liver.

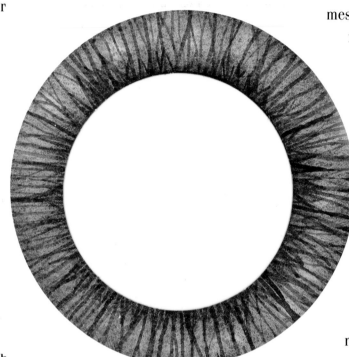

Intestine The tube linking the stomach to the rectum. The first part, called the small intestine, takes in nutrients from the digested food. The second part, the colon or large intestine, leads waste away to the rectum.

Mucus A thick, sticky liquid that coats the lining of many internal organs, including the oesophagus and stomach. It moistens them and protects them from damage.

Nerve A group of long, thin cells that carry messages between the brain and the rest of the body.

Nutrients Substances needed to fuel the cells so that they produce energy.

Organ A structure made of different kinds of cells which does a particular job in the body. The brain, stomach, liver and skin are all examples of organs.

Pancreas An organ that produces digestive enzymes and releases them into the intestine.

Peristalsis The squeezing action in the oesophagus, stomach and intestines which pushes the food along.

Protein A type of food which provides the material (amino acids) for building cells.

Spinal cord The thick bunch of nerves that runs from the brain down the back of the body.

Ureter The tube leading from the kidneys to the bladder.

Vein A tube that carries blood to the heart.

Villi Tiny, finger-like projections that line the inside of the small intestines.

Vitamin An essential chemical that the body needs—in small amounts—to function properly. A lack of, for example, Vitamin C, which is found in fresh fruit and vegetables, will lead to disease.